Homemade Adaptations for People with Disabilities

J. Rose Plaxen

SEVEN LOCKS PRESS

Santa Ana, California

Seven Locks Press
P.O. Box 25689
Santa Ana, CA 92799
(800) 354-5348

Individual Sales. This book is available through most bookstores or can be ordered directly from Seven Locks Press at the address above.

Quantity Sales. Special discounts are available on quantity purchases by corporations, associations, and others. For details, contact the "Special Sales Department" at the publisher's address above.

Printed in the United States of America

Library of Congress Cataloging-in-Publication Data
is available from the publisher
ISBN 1-931643-70-9

table of contents

introduction

Wouldn't if be great if children were born with a handbook? When you purchase a car, open the glove compartment and there is usually a handbook. It will always be there if you need to fall back on it. Unfortunately, a child does not come with a handbook. There are plenty of handbooks—or rather "home remedy" books—out there for the child without disabilities. But few for the child with disabilities.

Adapt My World features homemade adaptations, in recipe book form, for children with disabilities at home, school, and play. The concept of *Adapt My World* is clear: Simple adaptations at home, school, and play will help the child who is "differently-abled" achieve similar goals, tasks, and desires of the "able" child. A simple task, perhaps taken for granted, for a non-disabled child is often a challenge for the child with disabilities.

Having a child is one of the most wonderful experiences I have ever had. Daniel was born on the 4th of July, and boy did I see fireworks! He hit the typical milestones that you read about. Talk about retractable arms—no matter where I put things, Daniel could reach them. When Loren was born, I was excited to watch her develop into her youth as her brother did. Immediately, we knew she was different. Loren had medical issues and didn't even come close to any of her milestones. At 14 months, her neck could barely support her head. Crawling was even a chore for her. She was able to accomplish this, however, around her second birthday and take her first step at two-and-a-half years of age. Through early intervention, a wonderful team of therapist and simple adaptations, Loren was able to master early childhood tasks.

Adapt My World began when Loren was able to use a highchair. She needed help sitting up because she had low muscle tone and would slide out of the highchair. Therefore, she was unable to use a standard highchair successfully. One day, I went to the store looking for rubber strips for the tub. I decided to buy an extra set of strips and placed

introduction

them on the seat of Loren's highchair. For the first time, on her first birthday, she was able to sit with us at the dinner table with very little assistance. That's when I started cooking up ideas to adapt the world around Loren.

Adapt My World is first in offering simple modifications in many aspects of a child's life. Veteran parents, therapists, and teachers have handed down plenty of adaptations, of which few to none have been printed for public viewing. Now, families have a manual, full of knowledge, to guide them in accommodating their child's world. If you can follow a recipe, you should be able to follow this book. The adaptations—rather recipes—have ingredients, directions, and sometimes substitutes to make the preparation of the accommodations come to life.

Adapt My World focuses on home, school, and play. There are adaptations for mealtime, bathtime, bedtime, and dressing to make our children feel more independent in their home. You can find these in the "Home" chapter. Between independent and interactive play, there are several accommodations to allow these special children the opportunity to fit in. The "Play" chapter includes adaptations for all types of play, including sports and fitness. The "School" chapter has accommodations that have been developed by teachers and therapists so that a differently-abled child can study and socialize with their peers more efficiently. The wonderful thing about adaptations is that they can be carried throughout a child's day. What is done at home can be carried over to school and other activities throughout the day.

I hope that the flavor of *Adapt My World* encourages you to develop your own recipes.

shopping list

Most of us go to the grocery store with five items on our list and come home with twenty. Did you need *all* twenty items? No. Will you need them later? Perhaps. You probably bought the extra items because they were convenient to purchase at the time.

Here is a list of items that will be easily available to you for last-minute adaptations:

- Foam Curlers
- Velcro Fasteners
- Bungee Shoe Laces
- Bathroom Tissue
- Freezer Bags (quart or gallon)
- Glue
- Tape
- Drawer Knobs
- Index Cards
- Water Bottles
- 3-ring Binder
- Bathtub Strips

a note to reader

Adaptation Resource Network, Inc., Adapt My World, Inc., J. Rose Plaxen, and their employees assume no responsibility or liabilities for the adaptations contained in *Adapt My World.* An adult must assemble all adaptations contained in *Adapt My World.* The adaptations included in *Adapt My World* have been provided by individuals who generously donated (created or prepared) them in good faith. Adaptation Resource Network, Inc., Adapt My World, Inc., J. Rose Plaxen, and their employees assume no responsibility for successful use with all individuals with disabilities. Some adaptations are variations of the actual accommodations; therefore, there are alterations.

foreword

I guess, that in each person's life, there are lessons to be learned. For me, it is being taught courage, determination, and a mother's love by my youngest daughter, Joyce.

In her young life, she has found times more difficult than most have had to endure in an entire lifetime. In the last eleven years, she had to bear the tragic death of her first husband in a car accident, and taking onthe sole responsibility of raising two children. Daniel, her oldest child, was devastated by the loss of his father. He is now a senior in high school, thriving, and looking forward to college, thanks to the encouragement and counseling that his mother and "new" father are providing.

Loren, Joyce's youngest child, having been born with a cognitive disability, is epileptic. When a doctor told Joyce that her child would never walk, she spent most of her time learning what the problem was, and repeatedly spent what free time she had exercising and manipulating Loren's legs. Now Loren is an exceptional athlete participating in track and field events! When the child needed eyeglasses during her early years, she would not keep them on her head. Joyce found a shirt with an attached hood that prevented Loren from removing the glasses. Once the child found out that she could see better, she refused to have her glasses removed. Loren does not think of herself as being different from her friends, thanks to her mother. Joyce has necessarily had to improvise and modify everyday things, toys, eating utensils, shoes, zippers, etc., in order to meet Loren's everyday needs.

In school, Joyce has helped instructors, teachers, and students to understand what "disabled" means; and why the differently-abled need a bit more help to perform what most children can do easily.

Joyce goes that extra mile to help anyone with similar problems—with a smile on her face and a purpose in her stride.

Joyce's Mom

acknowledgements

I would like to thank Judith Devine, Judy Buckholtz, Faith Fischel, Suzanne Ripley, Jessica Taylor, Wayne Tart, Joanne Campbell, Lana Sedoti, Carolyn Owen, and Waverly Milor for their inspiring adaptations, suggestions, and/or assistance in adapting the world for people with disabilities. I would also like to express a special thank you to Photo Tech, for contributing the cover photos for the book, and John and Robyn Quinter, Quinter Design, for their guidance with the design of the book.

I also appreciate all the invaluable support from my family, friends and colleagues.

I look at life like a puzzle. Each aspect of your life is represented by a different piece of the puzzle.There are many pieces to make it complete and not all of the pieces are the same size. Nevertheless, each puzzle piece has a lot of importance, because they all belong to the "big picture."

This book is dedicated to Andrew, Daniel, and especially Loren. You make my puzzle complete!

play home school

play home school

introduction

This chapter focuses on home life, such as mealtime, bathtime, dressing, and more. You will find adaptations that help assist doing simple tasks that most children accomplish with little to no effort. I use adaptations at home to help Loren become more independent.

She likes to do things herself, which of course, builds self-esteem. First came the adaptation for the highchair, and then I wanted to adapt the world around my daughter. Every time Loren wanted to do something that was physically challenging for her, I would try to figure out a way to help her become self-reliant and part of the group. After coming home from therapy, Loren loved to get a snack and watch a video. While I was getting a snack for her, she would try to turn on the VCR. She would touch so many buttons that I could barely get the video to play. I realized that she is an independent thinker and wants to be self-reliant. That's when I started placing first-aid strips on electronics. I put a first-aid strip on the TV's "on" button and the VCR's "play" button. Loren was taught to only touch the first-aid strips and was able to independently watch her video. Doors have always been a challenge for her. Not until age 11 was Loren able to turn a doorknob. Prior to that the cylinders had to be omitted from doors throughout the house.

Simple alterations throughout your home will make life less challenging for you and your child.

Notes:

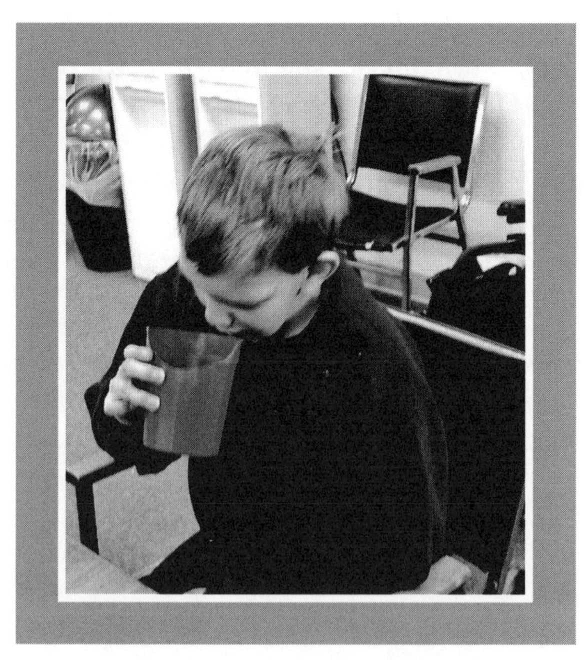

Cup

Most of us can tilt our head back and finish the last gulp of a drink. This modification is intended for the person who has difficulty achieving this task.

Plastic Cup (16 oz.)
Scissors
Sandpaper

First, take a pen and trace a line. The line should start at one edge of the cup, going down the side of the cup, and then finishing at the opposite edge. If this is done correctly, the line should look like half of a circle. Cut along the line carefully, making sure that there are no sharp edges. Sand to make smooth.

Notes:

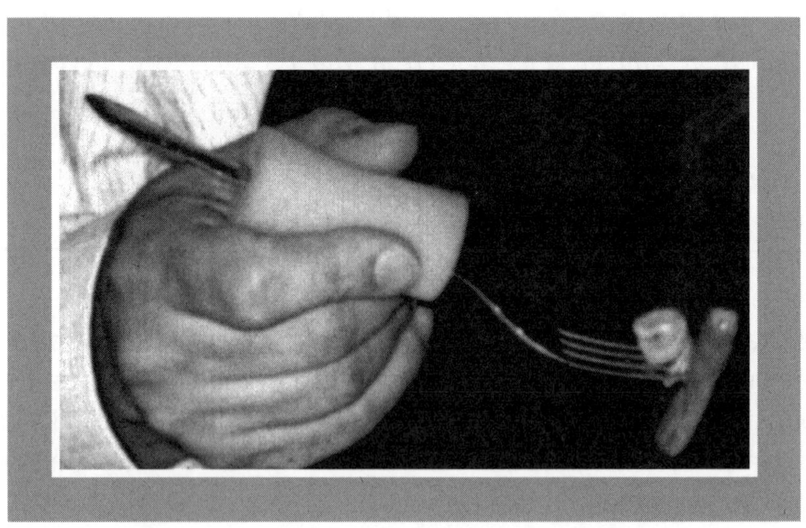

Fork Gripper

This is an ideal adaptation for the child that needs a wider grip on their fork.

Fork
Foam Curler

Place the fork in the center of the foam curler. Don't forget to throw out the plastic piece. Adjust the location of the curler according to where your child holds the fork.

Notes:

Knife

This is a unique way to cut things without a "typical" knife.

Pizza Cutter (dull)

A dull pizza knife can be used to cut anything soft, like pancakes, sandwiches, chicken, fish, etc.

Variation: Use a frosting knife. Make sure the cutting edge is dull.

Notes:

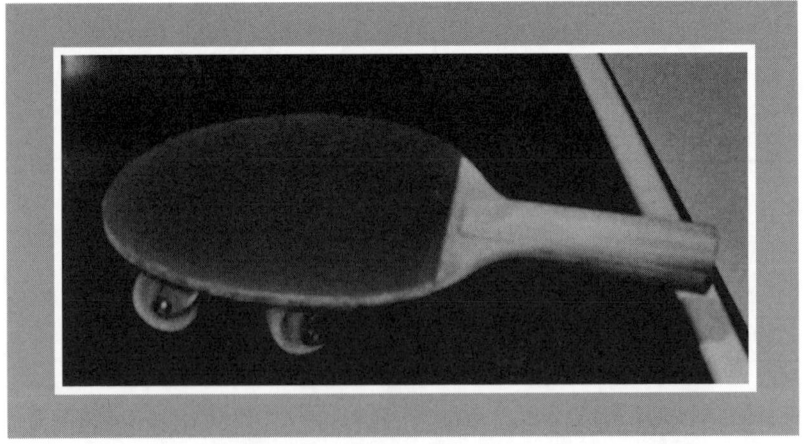

Trivet

Passing food around the table is easy with this. This trivet is great if you need to move things on the counter with only one hand.

Ping-pong Paddle
Square Oven Mitt
4 -Wheels (or dolly)

Attach square oven mitt to one side of ping-pong paddle. Attach wheels securely to the other side of the paddle.

Notes:

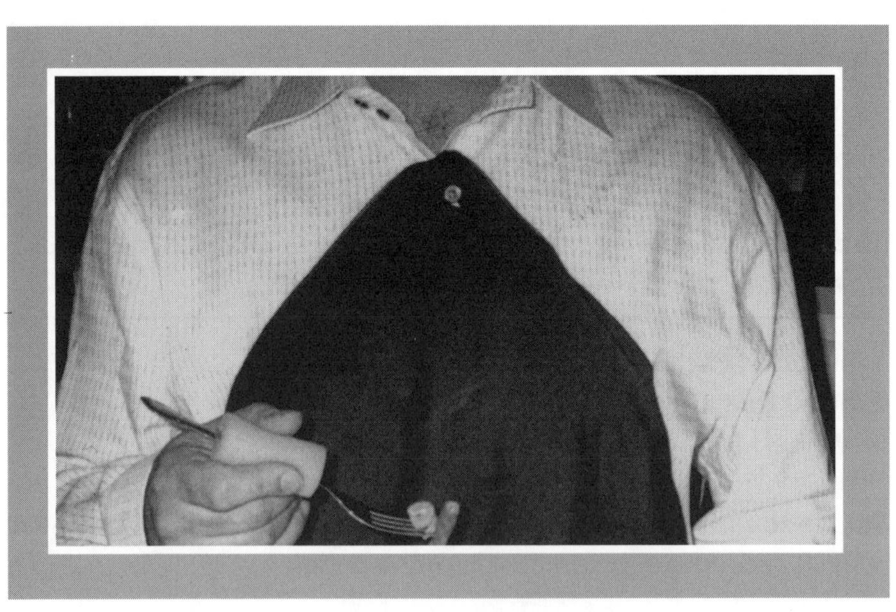

Button Napkin

This modification is a great way to keep clean at mealtime.

Cloth Napkin
Scissors

Take cloth napkin at one corner and make a "button hole." Attach napkin to a top button at the top of shirt. Spread napkin across body.

Notes:

Milk Bottle

Try this adaptation if pouring milk is a difficult task.

Pump Dispenser
Milk

Pour milk into a pump dispenser. Pump as much milk into your cereal as you would like.

Variation: This is wonderful to use with syrup for your pancakes.

Notes:

Utensils on a String

This adaptation will help eliminate utensils being dropped or thrown.

Utensils (fork or spoon)
Placemat
String (make tether)
Cloth Tape Measure

First, measure to determine the distance of the placemat from your child's mouth. Do not make string any longer then it needs to be. Make a hole towards the edge of the placemat. Attach one end of the string to the placemat and the other end of the string to the utensil.

Notes:

Placemat Placement

This idea will help avoid dishes being thown.

Placemat
Plate, Bowl, and/or Cup
1-inch, Adhesive-backed Velcro

Attach one side of the Velcro on plate, bowl, and/or cup.
Attach the other side of the Velcro on the placemat where desired.
Place plate, bowl, and/or cup on placemat on top of velcro.

Notes:

Stay Still Plate

It's very difficult to get food out of a bowl when the bowl moves from the force of the scooping. This might even work for the child who thinks it's funny to pick up his/her plate and throw it.

Placemat
Adhesive-backed Velcro
Plate and/or Bowl

Put one side of the Velcro on the bottom of the plate and/or bowl. Place the other side of the Velcro on the placemat (this may take some maneuvering). There you go—a plate and/or bowl that stay in place!

Notes:

Floor Protector

This modification is great! Your floor will stay clean.

Vinyl Tablecloth

Place a vinyl tablecloth under your child's chair.

Notes:

Placemat Magic

Setting the table is a breeze with this idea. This is a wonderful adaptation to assist a child with setting the table.

Solid-colored Placemats
Dark-color, Permanent Markers

Place a solid-colored placemat on the table. After placing plate, napkin, fork, knife, spoon, and/or cup on the placemat, outline the items with the marker.

Notes:

Pitcher

This adaptation creates an easy pitcher that is lightweight and unbreakable.

Milk Carton (quart)
Scissors

Cut off the top of the milk carton. Hold the carton by the handle to pour.

Notes:

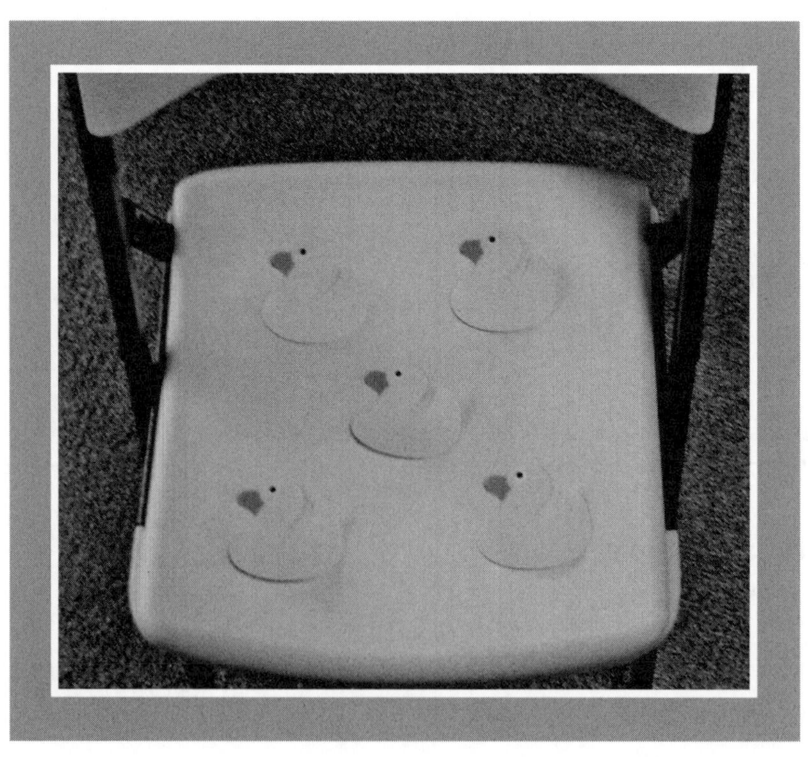

Non-slip Seat

Have you ever had trouble keeping your child with disabilities from slipping out of a highchair? Try this recipe.

Highchair
Rubber Jar Opener

Place rubber jar opener on seat of highchair, then strap your child in the highchair according to the manufacturer's instructions.

Variation: Use bathroom tub decals or strips in place of rubber jar opener on seat of highchair and strap child in according to the manufacturer's instructions.

Notes:

Snack Tray

The snack tray will help your child work on fine motor skills while having fun.

Ice Cube Tray
Snacks (cereal, nuts, raisins, etc.)

Place each snack in an individual section. Repeat with each compartment and a different snack.

Notes:

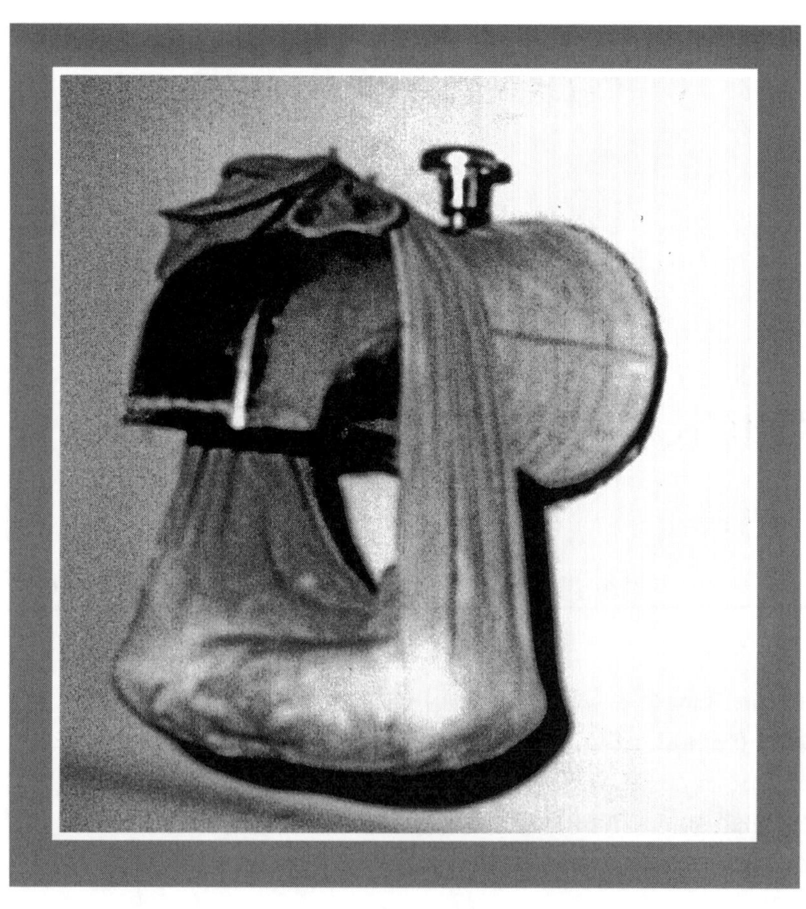

Soap on a Rope

Soap can be so slippery! This adaptation makes it easy to hold the soap. It won't slip out of your hands.

Bar of Soap
Knee-high Nylons

Take one of the knee-high nylons and insert the bar of soap—approximately halfway into the nylon. Tie the two ends together and lather up!

Notes:

Bathtime Goggles

This simple accommodation was a lifesaver for our daughter, who used to get shampoo and/or soap in her eyes while taking a bath.

Swim Goggles

Buy a pair of swim goggles and place overhead before the child takes a bath and/or shower. This will guarantee a fun bath time!! If your child wears glasses and has a hard time seeing without them, RX swim goggles are available.

Variation: A swim mask is as effective as the swim goggles.

Notes:

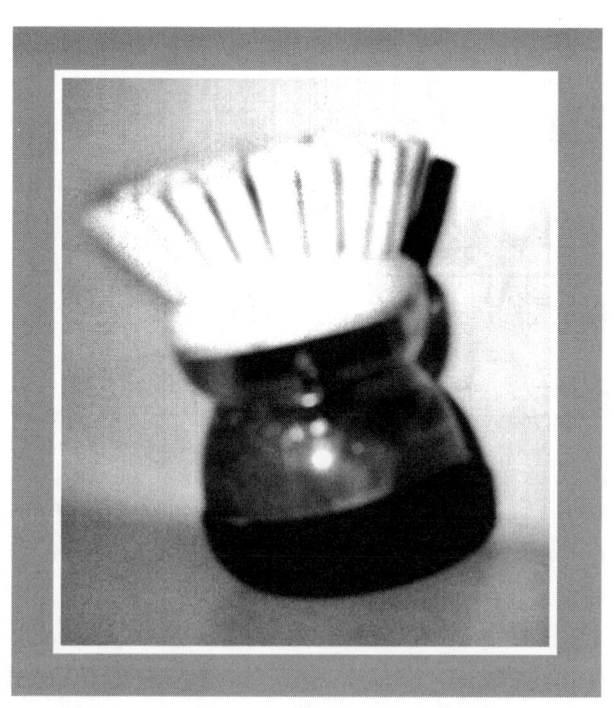

Washing Hair

This effective adaptation will assist in washing hair right down to the scalp.

Kitchen Scrubber
Shampoo

Open kitchen scrubber, pour shampoo into the opening, and close tightly. Place under the water to get wet and pump the dispenser at its opening. At this point, the shampoo will be out at the bristles. Before using on wet hair, make sure the shampoo is over the entire bristle area.

Notes:

Shower Visor

This is a surefire way to eliminate soap from getting in your child's eyes.

Plastic Visor

Place plastic visor on your child's head and start shampooing. The shampoo and suds will rinse off.

Notes:

Talking Reminder

This is a great way to remind a child to do a task.

Talking Picture Frame

Place a picture of a child doing a specific chore. For our daughter, it is turning off the light in her room. Follow the manufacturer's instructions to record a message. For example, "Lori, please turn off the light. Thanks!"

Notes:

Easy Door Opener

This adaptation will help the child with disabilities, who is unable to turn doorknobs, be able to enter a room.

Door
Screwdriver

Remove the lock on the door by removing the doorknob and replacing it without the lock.

Variations: Turn the door handle so the lock is not exposed and place duct tape over it. The door should not lock and should be able to pull open with ease.

Notes:

play home school

bath

Personal Hygiene Communication Board

Camera (preferably digital)
Paper (heavy stock)
Glue

Take photographs of your child doing a specific task, such as brushing teeth from the beginning to completion of the task. For example, putting toothpaste on toothbrush, brushing front teeth, etc.). Glue pictures on the paper, in order taken, and place near location of the task.

Notes:

On/Off Aide

First-aid strips aren't for boo-boos anymore!! You can see them on our televisions, VCRs, even our daughter's alarm clock (so she knows what button to turn off).

First-Aid Strips
Any Electronic Appliances or Devices

Place a first-aid strip on the "power" button of any electronic device. Your child will be able to turn the device off and on independently by easily locating the strip.

Variation: Instead of placing a first-aid strip, a dot of nail polish can be used.

Notes:

Alarm Clock

This simple modification will assist someone who cannot see the alarm clock to locate the on/off button or snooze button.

Alarm Clock
Adhesive-backed Velcro

Adhere the soft side of the Velcro tape to the snooze button and the rough side to the off/on button. Teach your child to identify each button by "feeling" and "seeing" it.

Notes:

Fishy Nightlight

This is not your typical nightlight!

Fish Tank with Light

Fill the fish tank with water, fish, plants, etc. and put it in the bedroom. When ready for lights out, turn on the "fishy nightlight." This is a relaxing way to have light in the room.

Variation: Use a lava lamp. Caution: A lava lamp can become hot to the touch.

Notes:

Open Closet

The doors on the closet can be very difficult to open. This is a surefire way to eliminate the problem.

Hammer

Take hammer and loosen hinges on the closet doors. Take door off hinges; remove door, exposing items in closet.

Notes:

Simple Clothing Adjustments

- Use **Velcro tape** on openings.
- Put **keychains on zipper tabs** to help pull down.
- Use **socks** that are too big so they are easier to put on and slouch down.
- Use **suspenders** instead of belts.

Notes:

Zipper Helper

This adaptation is used to help assist a child with disabilities with zipping up their own coat. You can also use this if the zipper foot of the coat breaks off.

Key Chain
Coat

Place a key chain on the zipper pull and there you have it!

Variation: A large paper clip or key ring can be used.

Notes:

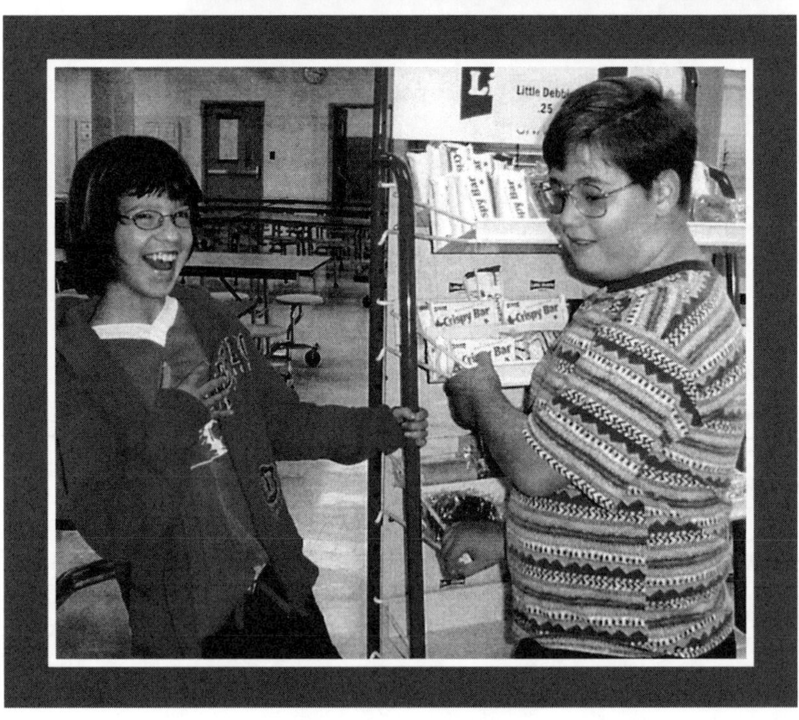

Bungee Pants

My daughter wants to wear jeans like her friends. Unfortunately, she can't properly use a button, limiting her choices of jeans. This is a great way to reach the goal of wearing jeans and being stylish, too!

Bungee Shoelaces
Scissors

Remove the button from the jeans. Place a small hole in the same spot, equal to the size from the existing button hole. Place the bungee shoelace through both holes, and pull slightly to tighten. No tying or buttoning!

Notes:

Jeans

Jeans (at least 1 size bigger than child's actual size)
Elastic

Buy jeans that are at least one size too big. Sew the elastic around the entire waistband after sewing up the zipper area.

Variation: This adaptation can be used on any type of pants.

Notes:

Creepy Leg Crawlers

This accommodation will help the differently-abled child crawl without their legs slipping out from under them.

Non-skid Socks
Scissors

Carefully cut the toes off a pair of non-skid socks. Place entire sock over child's leg, making sure the non-skid part is over the knee. The bottom of the sock gives your child the friction needed so they can crawl more successfully.

Notes:

Poncho Fun

Use this article of clothing instead of a regular winter coat.
For someone in a wheelchair, this is an easier way to put on a coat.

Large Fabric Square
Scissors

Trace a circle in the middle of the fabric, and cut it out.
Make sure the hole is big enough to put a head through.
Sew around the edges of the material. Place poncho over head and go!

Variations:

- Winter —use heavyweight material such as wool or heavyweight fleece.
- Raingear—use breathable waterproof material.
- Spring and/or Fall—use sweatshirt material.
- Summer—use lightweight material such as cotton.

Notes:

Bandana Bandit

When a child is a baby, they use a bib. When they are older and a child needs something to keep them clean and/or dry, what should you use? With this modification, a child with disabilities can keep their dignity and stay clean.

Bandana

Gently place and tie the bandana around your child's neck.

Variations: A scarf can be used.

Notes:

Wheelchair Arm Protectors

This will protect and cushion your child's arms.

2 Washcloths
Wheelchair
Duct Tape

Place a washcloth on the armrest of the chair. Attach with duct tape. Do the same on the other side.

Variation: Use fleece instead of washcloths.

Notes:

Walker Pouch

Trying to coordinate carrying items and using a walker can't be easy. Try this.

Basket for a Bicycle
Walker

This basket should have attachments already. Attach to the front of the walker.

Variation: A lunch pouch can be attached successfully.

Notes:

Dust Socks

Every child should take pride in their home and take an active role with cleaning it.

Socks (clean)

Put socks over your child's hands. Let them start to dust a tabletop, the television, or any surface that does not have breakables.

Notes:

Traveling Tray

This is great for travel. Items are less likely to fall.

Tray with Legs
Adhesive-backed Velcro
Plate, Cup with Lid, or Bowl

Place one side of the Velcro on plate, cup, etc. and the other side on the tray. Attach items where desired.

Notes:

Walker Grippers

This modification will provide a better grip while holding the sides of the walker.

2 Washcloths
Walker
Duct Tape

Place a washcloth on the handle of the walker. Attach with duct tape. Do the same on the other side.

Variation: Use fleece instead of washcloths.

Notes:

Double Bannister

A bannister is an important safety tool to navigate stairs. When one bannister is not enough, place another bannister on the other side. This will increase stability and security when using steps.

Bannister
Nails
Level

On opposite side from an existing bannister, install bannister along stairwell. Make sure it is the same height as the existing bannister. Use level and then nail in place. It must be properly secured to prevent possible injury.

Variation: Purchase bannister and have it installed professionally.

Notes:

home play school introduction

When you have children, you want to provide everything you had growing up and more. I couldn't wait to teach my kids how to play with blocks, puzzles, box games, tag, kickball, and more. Having a boy, I didn't know what to expect. I guess I thought he would play a sport, fix cars, and take out the trash. Having a girl was different. I myself remember playing with dolls, dancing, cheerleading, and playing with my stuffed animals with my sister.

When you have more than one child, you start comparing their "milestones," even with the knowledge that every child is different. With Daniel, he has always been a quick learner. He was able to stack blocks as high as he could reach and then karate kick them down. He relished in playing box games and strategically beating us. Daniel is now 18 and getting ready to go off to college. He would rather play electronic games than box games, and instead of blocks he stacks boxes. He would never karate kick them down because he knows he has to clean them up.

Loren has always enjoyed playing, but we needed to be a little creative with the preparations. Velcro tape on blocks, paper dolls, and any other toys that need balance is the way we found that she could participate in interactive and independent play. She can participate in some adaptive sports and activities. She liked playing with balls but would get frustrated when the ball would be thrown or kicked and then roll away. Now, we use a beach ball, put packing peanuts in it, and tape it closed. Loren likes to work out with me. She will try to lift my weights but finds it too difficult. Instead, she uses water bottles filled with water. The amount of water varies depending on how much she wants to lift. As a family, we enjoy and value our family time. We are able to expand this with puzzles, box games, and sports using a few homespun ideas.

This chapter will assist a child in all aspects of play. Every child wants to be a winner. Our children are no different—except the win for these special children is to participate, socialize, and challenge themselves—and then to triumph.

Notes:

Coloring Inside the Box

Coloring inside the lines is a breeze with this adaptation.

Glitter Glue (or colored glue)
Coloring Book

Apply glue to outlines of pictures in the coloring book. Let glue dry. Start coloring within the lines. The child will feel the outline of the picture and be encouraged to stay within the lines.

Notes:

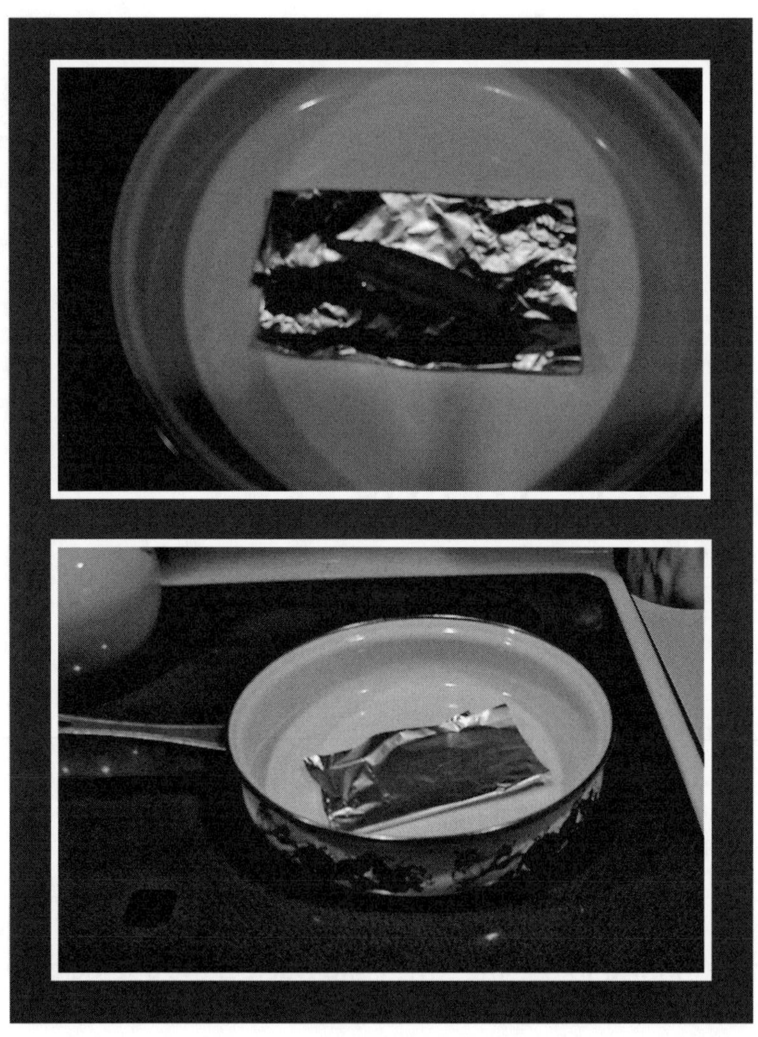

Crayon Melt

This adaptation prevents crayons from rolling away by flattening.

Crayons (preferably fat crayons)
Aluminum Foil
Pan
Stove

Remove paper label from crayon. Turn on a burner to low–medium heat. Place piece of foil on pan and one crayon on top of the foil. Place pan on burner for approximately 15 seconds to start. Remove when crayon is flat on one side. Allow crayon to cool and peel off the foil. Apply a fresh piece of foil for each crayon.

Warning: Do not walk away and/or leave the crayons on the stove without supervision.

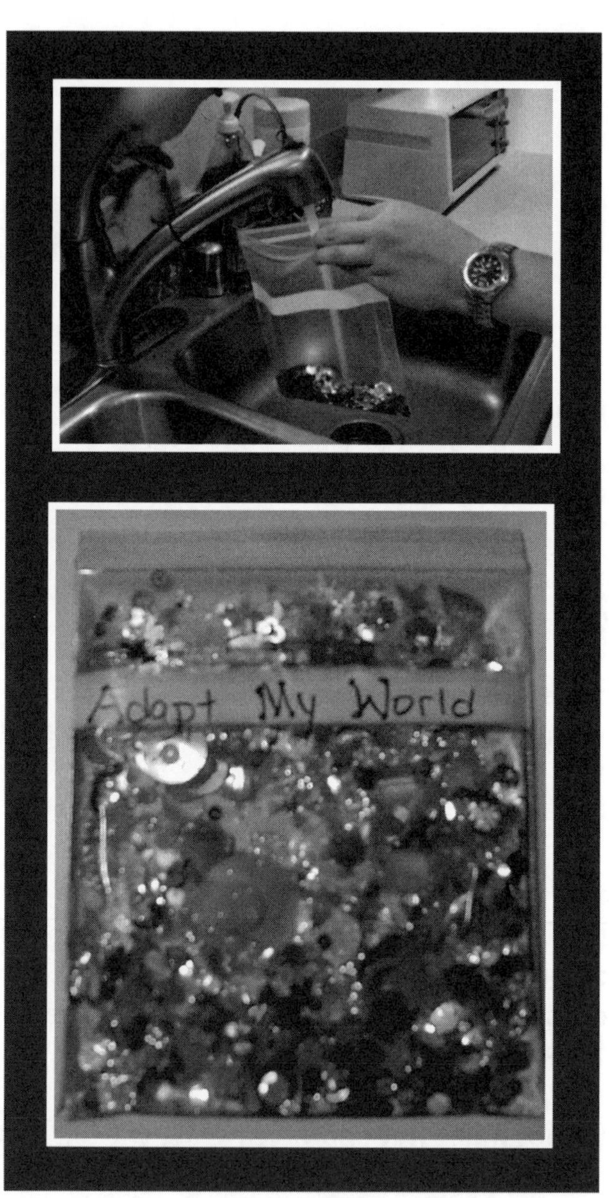
Adapt My World

Kaleidoscope in a Bag

This water bag will feel funny but will satisfy your child visually.

Gallon Zip Lock Bag
Water
Glitter
Beads
Glue

Fill bag half-to-three-quarters with water, glitter, beads, and anything else you would like to put in it. Adhere glue to zip lock. Zip closed. Let dry. Turn bag upside down to make sure the water doesn't come out. Place it on a flat surface. Your child can poke at it (gently) and see the materials move around.

Notes:

Puzzle Madness

Puzzles with handles can be very costly and somewhat difficult for a child who is differently-abled. This accommodation is going to make using a puzzle successful with little cost. The idea is to be able to place the puzzle pieces in the hole more accurately as well as using fine motor skills to pull the knob off the first puzzle piece and place it on the next.

Any Puzzle (with large independent pieces)
Adhesive-backed Velcro
Drawer Knobs (only 1 or 2 knobs are necessary)

Place one side of the Velcro on puzzle pieces and the matching side on the drawer knob. Place the drawer knob on the puzzle piece and put it where it belongs. Pull off the knob and repeat until the puzzle is complete.

Notes:

Easy Pouring Paint

Painting is a lot of fun, but can be messy. The following adaptation will allow for fun with very little mess.

Empty Hair Gel Container
Paint (non-toxic)

Make sure the hair gel container is clean and dry. Pour paint into container and replace lid tightly. No brush needed.

Notes:

Roller Paint

Painting with a roller can remove the mess without limiting the fun!

Empty Roll-on Deodorant Container (clean and dry)
Paint (non-toxic)

Remove the roller top of the deodorant container. Pour paint into the container, then place roller top back on securely. No brush is needed.

Notes:

Milk Carton Painting

This is a great way to apply paint to your project (instead of on you).

Small Milk Carton
Paint (non-toxic)
Paintbrush

Make sure the milk carton is empty, clean, and dry. Take a pen and puncture a hole on the side of the container. Pour paint into the top of the milk carton. Do not pour all the way to the top. Close the top of the milk carton and reinforce with tape. Now it's ready to be used. The paintbrush should fit into the hole so paint will not get all over the place.

Notes:

Paper Dolls I

Paper dolls come to life for a child with disabilities with this adaptation.

Paper Dolls
Adhesive-backed Velcro

Place Velco on the front of the doll and the back of all the clothes, hats, shoes, and accessories. If you wish, you may cut off the tabs since they are not needed.

Variation: If the paper dolls are laminated, they will not rip as easily.

Notes:

Paper Dolls II

Same concept as Paper Dolls I adaptation.

Paper Dolls
Small Magnets
Cookie Sheet

Place magnets on the dolls, clothes, hats, and accessories, which will all attach to the cookie sheet.

Variation: Place felt on the cookie sheet to add color.

Notes:

Wooden Fine Motor Board

Use this board to assist in learning method of opening and closing everyday items. Check it out.

Wood (make sure it's smooth, perhaps 10 inches by 10 inches; size will depend upon number of items used)
Zipper on Cloth
Doorknob
Light Switch
Door Latch
Glue (use glue gun) or Screw

Attach the ingredients to wood (your preference of attachment). Make sure all items are attached securely.

Notes:

Tray and Play

Your builder can be very successful stacking blocks with this idea.

Tray
Adhesive-backed Velcro
Blocks

Place one side of the Velcro on the tray.
Take the other side of the Velcro, place small pieces around the blocks, and start the fun! Your child can stack blocks on the tray without them falling easily.

Notes:

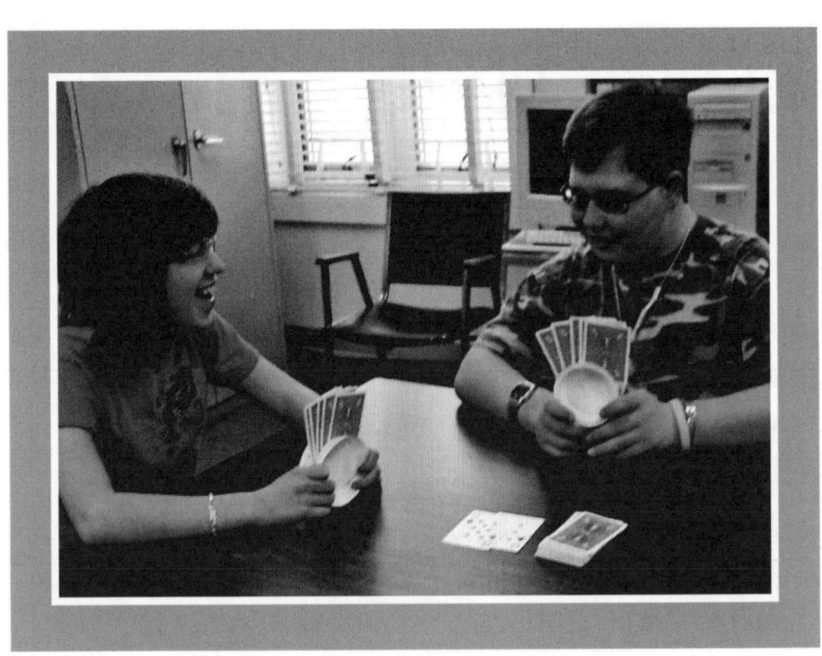

Card Holder

Everyone likes to play cards. This is a great adaptation that will help assist in holding the cards.

2 Plastic Hot Cup Lids
Glue

Place the two lids together, face to face. Place a large drop of glue between the two lids in the center. Allow to dry completely. The cards will fit between the lids.

Variation: Place the screw in the middle with nut.

Notes:

Bingo

Playing bingo is a lot of fun and educational, too.

Bingo Cards
Stamp

When your number is called, stamp with your favorite stamp.

Variation: The bingo cards can be made with index cards and your own numbers, letters, or even pictures.

Notes:

Sensory Play in a Box

So relaxing… you can explore various tactile materials.

Small Tub
Sand (or rice, dried beans, water, etc.)

Place the tub on a secured surface.
Put the tactile material (sand, rice, dried beans, water, or anything else you can think of) in the tub.
Start playing with the material with hands.

Variation: Place large tub or small sandbox on cement blocks. This will be easier to play without climbing in.

Warning: Small items may present a choking hazard for your child.

Notes:

Finger Painting Fun

This tasty approach to finger painting is a creative way to assist a child with pre-writing skills.

Table (preferably the kitchen table)
Whipped Cream

Clean table. Allow your child to "finger paint" using the whipped cream. A picture can be created, or they can write letters and/or numbers. Clean up is easy—just lick fingers.

Variation 1: Don't like whipped cream? Try pudding—let your child pick the flavor. Yogurt can be another yummy paint.

Variation 2: Shaving cream can be used, but DO NOT allow your child to lick fingers or place fingers in eyes!!

Notes:

Driving Games

For a child who is unable to hold a wheel, this adaptation will allow him/her to utilize a steering wheel for a computer and/or video game. Even a child without hands can steer to the finish line!
Caution: This adaptation is only used for a steering wheel for a computer game and/or video games only!

Steering Wheel (check with the manfacturer's instructions, making sure the wheel is compatible with computer or video equipment)
Cup (with an attachment to be used on a stroller)

Attach cup on the steering wheel. Place fist in cup and move in a circular motion to steer the game.

Notes:

Drums

There is no sound as sweet as drums in the kitchen while you're cooking!

Kitchen Pots
Wooden Spoons

Take pots and turn upside down. Use wooden spoons as drumsticks. Crank the music and regret that you ever showed your child how to make drums out of pots!

Variation: Pot lids can be used as cymbals, if you dare!

Notes:

Pool Painting

Doing this at the pool is a lot of fun!

Empty Diaper Wipe Container (with lid)
Paint Brush

Fill the diaper wipe container with water and start painting. Your child can "paint" on the sidewalk while practicing letters and numbers.

Notes:

Scavenger Hunt

This is a game that I remember playing when I was younger.

Paper Bag
Hidden Items
Index Cards
Photos/Pictures of Items

Mount the picture of each item in the scavenger hunt on an index card with the word printed below. This enables the child to participate in the hunt. Who's the most popular person in this game? The person holding the bag! Therefore, give the paper bag to a differently-abled person.

Variation: This can also be done in the grocery store by using a shopping cart instead of a bag.

Notes:

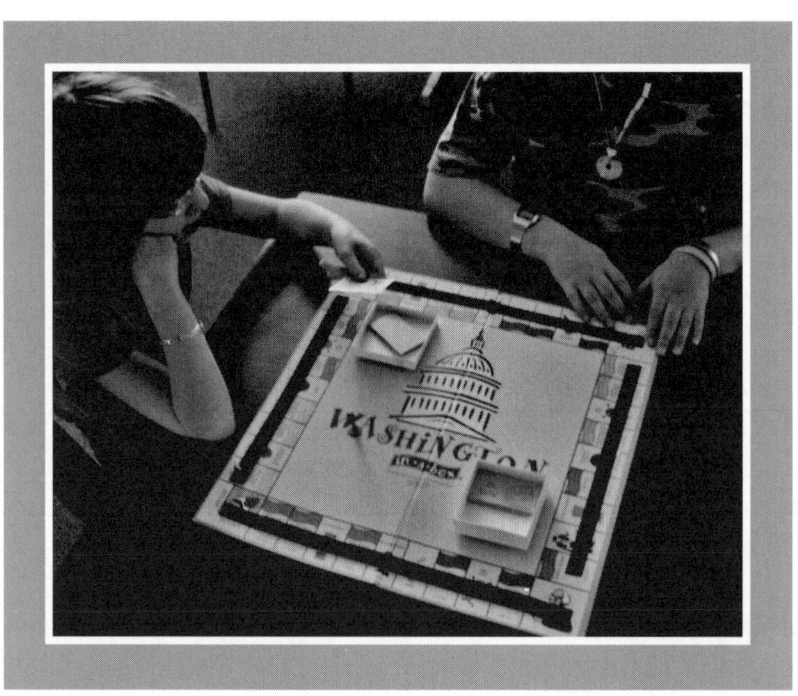

Board Game Fun

Using this accommodation will allow the board to have some movement without losing track of where the players are.

Board Game
Adhesive-backed Velcro
Small Cardboard Box (such as jewelry box)

Attach one side of the Velcro around the game board. Place the other side of the Velcro to the game pieces. Play the game using the manufacturer's rules.

Variation I: If the game includes cards to be placed on the board, attach small cardboard box, such as a jewelry box, to hold the cards.

Variation II: If throwing dice is difficult, use a small paper cup.

Notes:

High Visibility Cards

This will enable someone who has low vision or who is blind to play cards with a sighted partner.

Deck of Cards
Fluorescent Glue
Scissors

Clip the card on the upper left side. This will allow all players to be aware if the cards are upside down. Apply glue dots to the face of the cards. Allow to dry completely and start playing.

Notes:

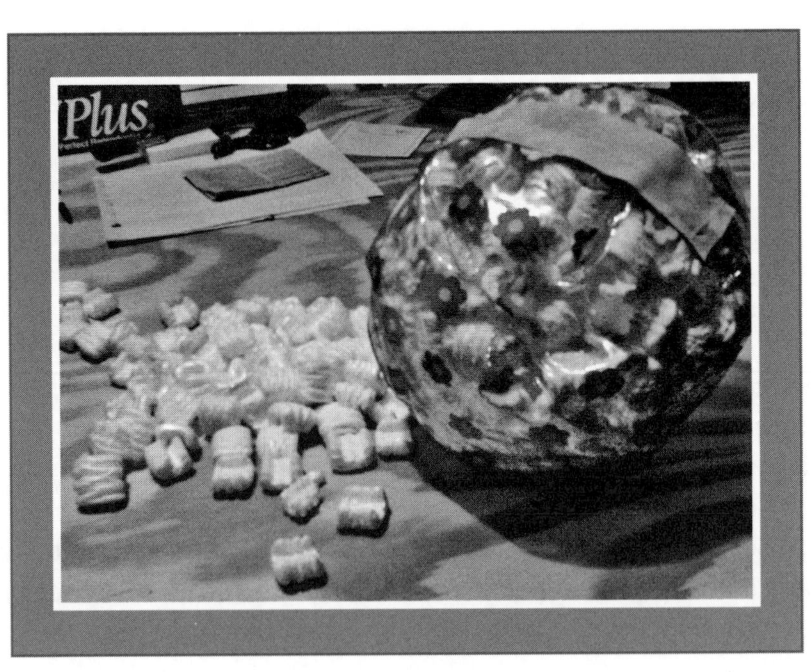

Ball Throw

Every child loves to throw or kick a ball. My daughter Loren was very frustrated with the ball because after being thrown, it would continue to roll away from her. After using this adaptation,when the ball was thrown and not caught, she didn't catch it; the ball would fall to the ground and stay there.

Beach Ball
Duct Tape
Packing Peanuts

Cut a hole in the ball, fill with the packing peanuts, and seal closed with the duct tape. (It may be helpful to glue the duct tape.) Feel free to throw and/or kick the ball.

Variation I: Most types of packing material can be used.

Variation II: Add bells before sealing with tape. This will allow someone with low vision to hear the ball.

Notes:

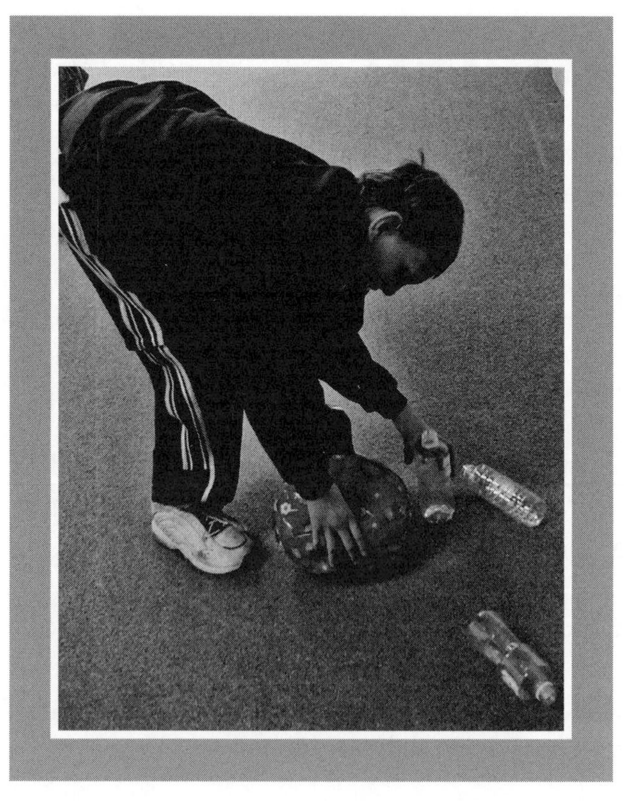

Bowling Fun

Children of all ages like bowling! Where else can you throw something, see the pins explode, and you don't have to clean it up?? Bowling can be difficult. The balls are heavy and the pins are far away. This adaptation was forwarded by a Certified Adaptive Physical Education Specialist.

Ball (see Ball Throw on p.133)
8 - 10 Plastic Bottles

Follow "Ball Throw" recipe. Fill plastic bottles with water. You can fill the water with dye for color recognition. The bottles can also be filled with less water so they'll fall more easily.

Variation: Other balls, such as a rubber ball, can be used; however, using a hard ball is not suggested.

Notes:

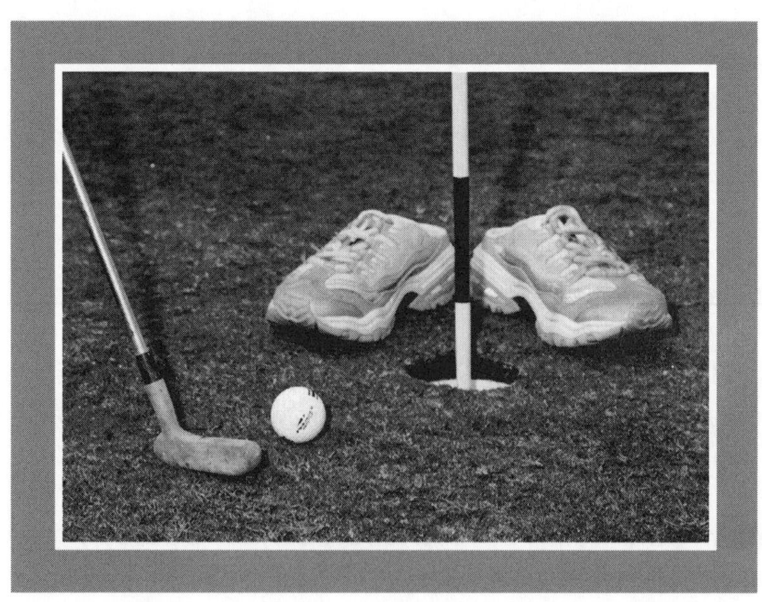

Putt Putt Golf

This is a "shoe-in" adaptation. Any golfer would love this adaptation!!

Golf Hole
Shoes (pick a style that's flat)

Place the shoes at the hole. The heels of the shoes should be touching and the toes apart, to either side of the hole. The shoes should look like a "V." Aim and putt the ball. If done correctly, the ball should easily go in the hole.

Notes:

Paddle Ball

This can be used for a child who needs a larger paddle or racket.

Hanger
Plastic Wrap
Foam Curler
Tape

Reshape the hanger so the body of the hanger is open in a circle. Cover the circle with plastic wrap, with the plastic wrap gathered at the twisted base of the hanger. Tape securely.
Take foam curler and cover the hook portion.
A child can use it to hit a ping-pong, tennis, and/or beach ball.

Notes:

Relay Batons

This is a great hand-eye coordination game.

Cardboard Tube (from center of paper towels)

Have one child hand off the "baton" to another child. The children should be positioned a few feet apart when passing the "baton." Let the games begin!

Notes:

Water Weights

This is a great way for your child to participate in lifting light weights.

Two 1-pint Plastic Bottles of Water
Food Coloring
Water

Fill both water bottles with the same amount of water. We started off with very little water in the bottles, so our daughter felt successful immediately. Just add food coloring and seal top securely.

Caution: Check with the doctor before starting any weight-lifting activity.

Notes:

Terry Water Holders

After playing hard, a refreshing drink hits the spot. With this holder, the moisture is absorbed, and the water bottle is less likely to slip.

1-Pint Water Bottle
Terrycloth Wristband

Stretch wristband over the side of the water bottle.

Notes:

home school play

introduction

Children are unique, and watching them develop is a tremendous experience. Our son was in pre-school around his third birthday. He was developing fast and delighted in learning. He consumed the socialization, and we enjoyed watching him thrive socially and educationally.

We approached our daughter differently. Loren entered into the Infant and Toddler Program after her first birthday. She received physical and occupational therapy, speech/language, and education. Loren was overwhelmed, at times, with the demands of therapy, learning, and social interactions. Overall, she did enjoy going to school. By kindergarten, she was going to school all day. She would be in A.M. kindergarten, have lunch, and then go to class with her buddies in the community-based program. The kindergarten class was the first time Loren was educated with peers that were non-disabled. We started to make simple accommodations. She would place her backpack and coat in a bin instead of hanging them up like the other kids. A stamp, with Loren's name on it, was used for her to put her name on her work. It was a wonderful adaptation for Loren to become independent and have the ability of "writing" her name on class work. The teacher worked with us and made up accommodations as she went along.

Through the years, Loren has always been in a community-based program and mainstreamed into "regular" classes. She still enjoys being with her non-disabled friends and does receive assistance from a teacher in the classroom. Her ability to understand what she is learning is tremendous! She needs prompting to get to know the knowledge she possesses. Now, at 15 years of age and in high school, Loren is known at school and the community as "Lori." She started to call herself that and her friends know her by that name. In essence, she has adapted her name. She has become very independent and loves going to school.

The "School" chapter helps a child with disabilities fit in by offering adaptations with positioning, writing, self-care, and more.

Notes:

Pencil Gripper

I can tell you that we had a very difficult time finding an accommodation to assist our daughter, until we identified this. This adaptation is used for the child who needs a pencil grip to be fatter.

Pencil
Foam Curler

Place the pencil in the middle of the foam curler (there should already be a hole through the middle). Don't forget to throw out the plastic piece. Adjust the placement of the curler according to where your child holds the pencil.

Variations: Yes, I'm sure there are plenty.

Notes:

Name Stamp

Every child should get credit for the work completed. Some of our kids have a very difficult time with their writing skills. A name stamp will give a child with disabilities the ability to put their name on their papers.

Self-inking Stamp (with child's name on it)

In the place where the name is to be written, just stamp. Using a self-inking stamp is the best approach to this adaptation. Otherwise, see "Stamp Surprise" adaptation, which follows.

Notes:

Stamp Surprise

Children love to use stamps and ink pads. Sometimes the stamps are difficult to hold. This adaptation is used to assist a child with disabilities.

Stamps
Stamp Pad
Knobs (from drawers)
Adhesive-backed Velcro

Cut a small piece of Velcro to fit on the stamps to be used. Place the other side of the Velcro on each drawer knob. Have a great time creating!

Notes:

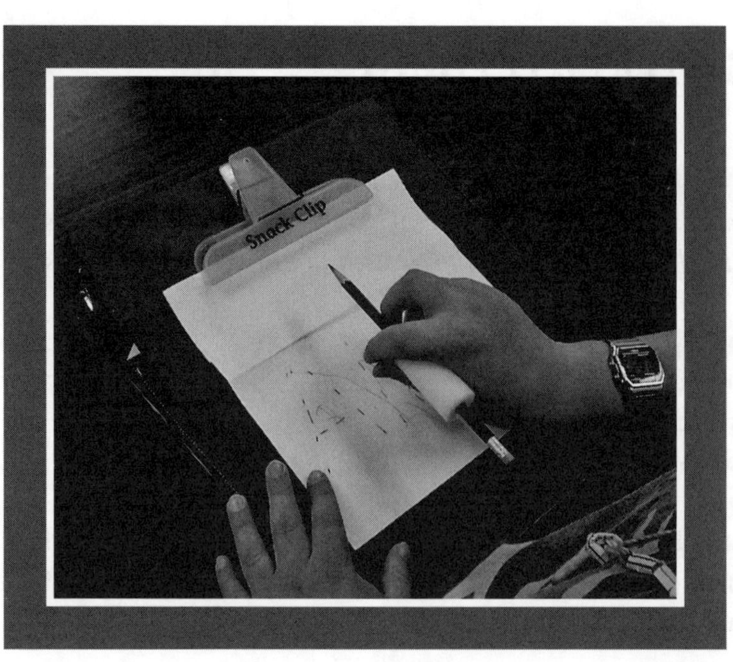

Slant Board

The concept behind using a slant board is to make it easier to write. The added bonus is that the paper will be clipped at the top and won't slip. This is great to use if the child is in a wheelchair.

3-inch, 3-ring Looseleaf Binder
Large Clip (as designed for bags of chips)
Glue

Position the binder on a table in front of you. If this is correct, the 3-ring binder should be on its side, sloping towards you. Glue clip to the top of the binder.

Variation: The use of a 1-inch or 2-inch binder is acceptable.

Notes:

Pre-writing Skill

This wonderful method is used when teaching a child with disabilities to follow a line. The raised glue will work as a guide against which to glide the pencil.

Glitter Glue (colored glue)
Paper
Pencil

Apply the glue, on the paper, in a line across the page. You can do this several times in any direction. After the glue has completely dried, your child will take the pencil and place the point against one end of the glued line and continue to the other side of the line.

Notes:

Reading Guide I

A reading guide is a terrific way to maintain a child's focus on the material.

Index Card
Reading Material

Place the index card under the words being read.

Notes:

Reading Guide II

This is an accommodation of Reading Guide I.

Index Card
Scissors

Cut out a horizontal, oblong hole in the index card, leaving an edge of approximately ¼-inch on either side. This will enable a person to more easily see smaller print.

Notes:

Magnifying Print

Using this adaptation will perhaps enable someone to see their reading material more clearly.

Magnifying Glass
Reading Material

Hold the magnifying glass against your reading material. This will enable a person to more easily see smaller print.

Notes:

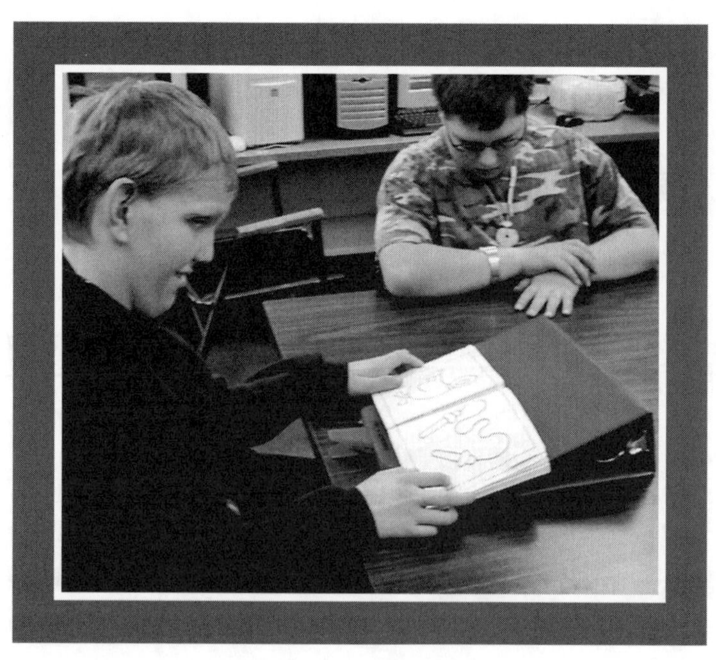

Reader's Slant Board

This follows the same concept as the previous Slant Board adaptation, but with a twist. Holding a book and turning the pages can be a challenge. This modification will allow the reader to rest the book.

3-inch, 3-ring Looseleaf Binder
Clip (as designed for bags of chips)
Glue

Position the binder as you would the Slant Board adaptation previously discussed, with the slope towards you. Position the clip at the lowest part of the binder, and glue. Place the book above the clip. If the book is fairly thin, it can be clipped at the bottom for

Notes:

Positioning Pleaser I

Most kids squirm in their chairs. For our kids, positioning is a very important skill, which is needed to successfully sit in class. This accommodation will give a child a place for their feet.

Block
Chair

Position the block under the chair so the child's feet rest on top of the block. This prevents the child's feet from dangling and provides a firm placement of the feet beneath the chair.

Notes:

Positioning Pleaser II

This adaptation was used for our daughter Loren. When sitting in an average school chair, there was a lot of room between her and the desk. With this accommodation, she is able to sit closer to her desk and not squirm.

Furniture Cushion (an outdoor furniture cushion can be used)
Chair

Place the cushion on the chair—either on the back, on the seat, or both.

Variation: A pillow will accomplish the same goal in a pinch!

Notes:

Foot Rests

A key to positioning is that your feet are firmly on the floor. This will allow for less fidgeting. If the child's feet do not touch the floor, this is a fantastic way to adapt.

Phone Books

Place phone books on floor and plant feet on them.

Variation: Place the phone books on the floorboard of a car for positioning.

Notes:

Positioning Seat Ring

This reminds me of the "donuts" used after having a baby. Very effective to place a child in the seat.

Child's Inflatable Swimming Ring
Chair

Inflate inner tube until almost tight, leaving it slightly limp. Place inner tube on seat. Have the child sit in the middle of the inner tube so the tube surrounds their "seat."

Notes:

Clean Face

Here's a fun way to get a child to keep their face and hands clean at the table. People with sensory issues have a difficult time because they often cannot feel the food or crumbs on their faces. Our daughter has been using this "clean face" method for several years now. Even her non-disabled peers bring in a mirror to look at themselves at the end of lunch!

Pocket Mirror

Have the child bring the mirror to the lunchroom and pull it out before eating. They can bring it in their lunchbox or carry it in their hand. After eating a few bites, look in the mirror and dust away the crumbs.

Variation I: Use a free-standing mirror, as seen in the picture.

Variation II: Attach a free-standing mirror to the wall next to the table.

Variation III: Glue a mirror on the inside of the lunchbox.

Notes:

Homework Helper

Getting your child to get their homework done can be very taxing. Try this way of motivating your child to do their homework or chores.

Paper Gift Bag
3-inch x 3-inch piece of paper

On each piece of paper, write down a different activity or "prize" that they will enjoy earning. You can choose to let them play with their toys or even watch a half hour of their favorite television show. Fold the piece of paper and place in the bag. After completing homework, let them pull out a folded paper and read the prize.

Variation: A spin wheel can be used instead of the paper and bag. Write on the spin wheel the different homework awards and let the child spin the wheel to select his/her reward.

Notes:

Drinkable Carton

Have you ever seen a child use a straw in a carton of milk and tilt it slightly? It goes all over the place. With this adaptation, the carton of milk is used… with less mess.

Milk Carton
Straw
Pen

Take a clean pen and poke through the side of the carton of milk. Make sure the puncture is high enough so milk doesn't come out. Place straw in hole so your child can enjoy their milk.

Notes:

Paper Holder

This will enable a child, who is only able to use one hand, cut more effectively.

Wood (2 inches x 4 inches for top)
Wood (6 inches x 4 inches for bottom)
Clothespin
Wood Glue

Create an upside down "T" shape by gluing wood pieces together with the 6-inch x 4-inch board positioned horizontally and the 2-inch x 4-inch piece centered vertically. Glue the clothespin to the top of the 2-inch x 4-inch piece. Place paper in clothespin. Holding the paper is now much easier.

Notes:

Non-slip Ruler

Drawing a straight line is easier said than done. With this adaptation, a straight line will be completed more easily.

12-inch Ruler
Cabinet Knob
Glue
Caulk

Glue the knob to the top of the ruler at the 6-inch mark. Apply a strip of caulk to the bottom of the ruler. The ruler will be ready to use after the caulk has dried completely.

Variation: Don't have a spare cabinet knob? Try using a spool, less the thread, affixing it with glue.